Hooking Rugs

Storey Publishing

Hooking Rugs

Lila Fretz

CONTENTS

Introduction & Brief History

Men, women, young and old—all can hook. The manual dexterity and keen eyesight required for some needlecrafts are unnecessary for rug hooking. Learning one easy stitch makes it possible to hook any design. There is no threading of a needle, no counting of fine threads, and no elaborate finishing procedures. Of all needlecrafts, rug hooking is one of the least expensive, easiest, and yet most creative. In the past even the hook was handmade from a nail and given a wooden handle. Be prepared to take some good-natured kidding when you tell your friends you're a "hooker."

Possibly the earliest sample of hooking was done by the Vikings in the Bronze Age. It is on display in the Oslo Museum in Norway. Much later rug hooking using wool yarns surfaced in England, a country with an active textile industry. North American rug hooking with wool materials was first done in coastal areas, mainly New England, Nova Scotia, and Canada, where the craft was introduced by sailors and settlers from Europe. Slowly the craft spread to rural areas of the East and Midwest United States.

Textiles, being extremely time-consuming and later expensive to make, were never discarded. Heeding the old New England saying, "Use it up, wear it out, make it do, do without," hooking provided a use for material too worn for any other purpose.

Rugs were also hooked for warmth. The first rugs, "bed ruggs," were used on beds. Later most rugs were used on the dirt and board floors to ward off chills.

Finally, there was a longing for beauty in a household where only the essentials were considered important. The early housewife could draw her own design on linen with charcoal, use worn-out clothing "as is," or overdye her wools with leaves, berries, and wildflowers for different colors, unwittingly creating a folk art that now helps to tell the story of our ancestors and their times.

Rug hooking became very popular during the middle to late 1800s. Traveling as a tin peddler near Biddeford, Maine, Civil War veteran Edward S. Frost saw women struggling to create designs. A good businessman, he saw a way to help. In 1868 Frost made the first metal stencil of his own design from an old tin boiler, and printed the design on burlap. He sold these preprinted patterns to eager customers, dealing a blow to the originality of hooked rug folk art. However, the patterns themselves are now considered folk art. Some of the original stencils are owned by the Henry Ford Museum in Dearborn, Michigan.

Traditionally hooking was done only to make rugs. Now there are many uses including covered brick doorstops, pads and coasters for tables, wall hangings, stool covers, chair pads, pillows, handbags, etc. Your imagination may offer still others.

There are several different types of hooking:

Primitive: Historically, this described rugs made of wide strips cut with a scissors, with little realistic detail in the motifs, and unsophisticated coloring. The term is still used today even if the wide strips are cut with a mechanical wool strip cutter and the pattern is a commercial one. Primitive hooking is done with ¼-inch and wider strips of all kinds of wool. The design can be old-fashioned or contemporary. The wide widths of the strips limit the small detail in the motifs, but shape and interest is achieved with very simple shading and highlights. Outline and fill hooking is very popular in primitive rugs. There is much room in these rugs for fun and originality.

Realistic: With the invention of the wool strip cutter, it is possible to cut a strip of wool ³⁄₃₂-inch wide. With strips this narrow, hooking truly becomes "painting with wool." A petal of a rose may have six to eight graduated values of a color fingered or blended so that the rose looks lifelike. To get the graduated shades necessary for this type of hooking, all white wool must be used, and strict dye formulas followed. While it is a challenge to do this successfully, the birds, flowers, and animals do look real.

Pictorial: Pictorial hooking is similar to landscape painting. It can be a farm scene, a covered bridge, a neighborhood, or an animal family. Pictorials can be done with wide strips in the primitive style, with large motifs and less detail, or with narrow strips and much more detail for realism. A combination of wide and narrow strips can also be used for different effects.

Geometrics: An arrangement of squares, triangles, diamonds, stars, hexagons, or circles hooked individually or in combination with each other is repeated over the surface of the rug. These shapes can be alternated with flowers or leaves. Easy to design with a ruler and compass, these are good rugs for beginners. Any width of strip can be used.

Waldoboro: Waldoboro hooking forms a deep pile, which is cut and sculptured to make the design (usually flowers) appear three-dimensional. Named after the town of Waldoboro, Maine, where the custom originated, these rugs are hooked with narrow strips. Being very impractical to walk on, they are mainly used as decorative wall hangings.

Getting Started

Supplies

burlap or monk's cloth backing: In the past, and still today in rural areas, burlap feed bags were opened to their full size and used for rug backing. Today good-quality Scottish burlap can be purchased by the yard in 48-inch and 60-inch widths suitable for the wide woolen strips of primitive hooking. Monk's cloth is an even-weave natural-colored cotton backing available in 72-inch and 144-inch widths. A good selection for a very large rug or a hall runner, it is suitable for wide- or narrow-cut strips.

hand hook: The hook should be a primitive or coarse hook. A crochet hook will do in a pinch.

thumb tacks: ½-inch long

scissors: Sharp cloth cutting scissors are a must to cut ¼-inch wool strips.

felt-tip pen

needle and thread: Carpet thread and a strong needle are necessary to sew back the tape binding when the rug is finished.

frame: The frame can be a 14-inch embroidery hoop or a quilting hoop on legs. I like a wooden frame to which the pattern is attached with tacks. This wooden frame can be made from four pieces of pine nailed together or canvas stretchers (found in art supply stores). The frame can be attached to a table with a C-clamp, or legs can be attached to the frame. Make sure the depth of the frame does not exceed your reach, as one arm works under the frame and the other works on the top.

nonadhesive 1¼-inch twill tape binding

wools: the most important part! More on that in the section on wools.

Optional

mechanical wool strip cutter: A small hand-operated machine that cuts wool into strips from 3/32-inch wide to 1/4-inch wide by changing the blade.

textile dyes: A great deal of fun can be had with Cushing's Perfection Dyes for wool. These dependable, colorfast, commercial dyes come in a wide range of colors and add a new dimension to your hooking.

bent handle rug shears: These are offset handled scissors with a beveled point that enables the hand to get closer to the flat hooking surface while cutting the end of the hooking strips.

All equipment suggested can be purchased from the suppliers listed on page 30. These suppliers are also very helpful with your questions about hooking supplies.

Wools

At first it will seem you will never have enough wools to hook, and the temptation to purchase new wool will be great. Resist the temptation, as new wool is very expensive, and using all the same material can be boring to hook and to look at. Remember this is a needlecraft historically done with recycled materials. See what wools you can scrounge from neighbors, family, thrift shops, flea markets, leftovers from sewing projects, etc. Put out the word about your new needlecraft, and gifts of wools will trickle in, slowly at first, but gaining momentum as friends catch the spirit. You will be given much material of doubtful parentage. Take it all so as not to offend. You can weed out cotton and synthetic materials in private. To test for wool, a tip of doubtful material can be burned with a match. Burning wool smells like burning hair. A small percentage of synthetic fiber in a piece of wool will not affect the wearability or looks of a rug, but do not use 100% cotton or 100% synthetic materials because their dirt-resistance and wearability characteristics are too unlike wool.

Preparing Wools

All types of wool (tweeds, textures, solids, lights, and darks) are useful. Dismantle each garment and discard unusable pieces. For wool to be usable it must be at least 4 inches long and on the straight of the grain. It is tedious to hook with short 4-inch strips, but not impossible. Strips 10 to 15 inches long are preferable. Wash and dry the usable pieces. If the wools are the colors you desire, they can now be cut into strips ¼ inch wide if medium weight, narrower if heavy weight wools. If wool materials are light weight, cut ½-inch wide. These ½-inch-wide strips will be held folded double as you hook them. Avoid hooking with loose-weave wool in your first project. Save this for a second project as it requires a more experienced hand.

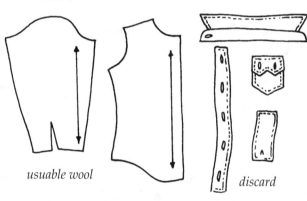

usuable wool

discard

Always cut strips on the straight of the grain. Never cut on the bias. Strips cut diagonally will quickly pull apart. All wool material can be torn on the straight of the grain. A closely woven flannel can be torn as narrow as ½ inch. To keep cutting on the grain, periodically tear the wool piece you are using to get back to the straight of the grain. When cutting your strips with a scissors, cut a strip twice as wide as you want, then carefully cut in half. It is easier than cutting one narrow strip from a large piece of wool. Moth holes do not matter in the wool. Cut around them. A 12-inch strip hooks a line approximately 3 inches long. Do not cut all your wool into strips at once. It may not be needed. Cut as you hook or keep a little ahead. On the other hand, do not waste or throw out "too small" pieces of wool. You may be desperate for them later.

To determine the amount of wool necessary to hook a given area, layer the area to be hooked with the wool folded into five thicknesses. It takes roughly five times the area to be hooked. For large areas, a general rule is: ½ pound of wool to hook 1 square foot of burlap.

Selecting or Creating a Design

Excitement! That is what is necessary to complete a hooked rug. Start with something you like. Resist the temptation to finish someone else's partially worked rug. Aunt Sadie may have been famous for her pumpkin pies, but not for her sense of design and color harmonies. Usually the half-finished rug has spent the past fifteen years stored in a hot, dry attic and has become dried out and brittle, a factor limiting its life span before you even begin to hook. Remember, it takes as much time to hook a poor design as it does to hook one you like. This is an opportunity to make your own design statement.

First decide where you will place the rug. A one-way design works well in front of a fireplace or a piece of furniture. A rug to be viewed from all sides must have no top or bottom or direction within its design. A half-round "Welcome" rug is particularly pleasing at entries. A pictorial-scene makes a nice wall hanging.

Also consider size. One side one and one-half times the length of the other side is a pleasing proportion. A square rug can be more difficult for the beginner to design. Avoid choosing a size too small in order to finish quickly. It may look skimpy and not give the satisfaction of a larger rug. If you want to learn on a smaller project, choose a chair pad or pillow. Here your individuality can speak out with less time consumed.

Many designs can be found in commercial patterns available at the suppliers listed on page 30. The designs are varied and printed on good-quality burlap. But consider creating your own design even if you think you lack artistic ability. Design ideas are everywhere: paper snowflakes, greeting cards, primitive ethnic designs such as Pennsylvania Dutch motifs, astrological and church symbols, children's coloring books (already simplified), weathervanes, needlework patterns, leaves, children's drawings, wrapping paper, and quilts, to name a few.

Repeating patterns are easier for the beginner, as are Pennsylvania Dutch motifs where one half of the rug is a mirror image of the other half. Designs based on the square, diamond, triangle, circle, or circle within a square, can be marked out easily with a ruler and a compass (or even a plate or cup). These geometrics are particularly effective in hooked rugs. Alternating squares with a design of leaves or flowers is also fun. The combinations are endless. A small rug with a family pet as the central figure could be your basic design with a colorful border of squares or scallops to complete the design.

For an original design, you will need plain backing. The amount of burlap or monk's cloth to purchase for your rug is determined by the size of your rug plus at least 6 inches on every side for attaching the backing to the frame.

Leave space for a border on your rug, but hook it last. Your design may not need one. Border color also depends on the colors used in your design motifs. A light, airy design needs a narrow border. A heavy, bold design can use a wider border. Designs without borders tend to advance or project; designs with a border tend to recede or draw back.

Designing Guidelines

- Choose a dominant theme such as a geometric, or a specific center of interest such as a sleeping cat or a vase of flowers.
- Balance motifs on the backing so one end of the rug does not appear heavier than the other.
- Avoid small details; your rug will appear cluttered. Also ¼-inch-wide strips limit the amount of detail possible.
- Leave some space around your design motifs. "Leave room for the bird to fly," as the saying goes.

Applying the Design to the Backing

When you have determined the size of your rug, you must decide on the size of the motifs to be used in the design. Consider the space necessary for background around flowers and hearts and other shapes. Motifs should not be crowded, but neither should they be floating in too much space. A good way to see if your design is pleasing is to cut out rough paper shapes of your motifs. Place the cutouts on the backing within the rug outline, allowing space for the border. You may decide to change the size or placement of the motifs, or perhaps use different designs around the edge instead of a solid border.

Designs can be enlarged by using an enlarging copier or by using graph paper. When using graph paper, first trace the motif onto ½-inch grid graph paper by holding the drawing and the graph paper up to the window. The light enables you to see the drawing through the paper, and the glass gives you a hard surface on which to trace. Next choose a paper the size you wish the finished motif to be. Divide the larger paper into the same number of grid lines as the smaller traced motif. Draw, square by square, the motif as you see it on the smaller grid.

This motif can be transferred to the backing by using a hot iron and a transfer pencil, or by placing nylon net or a thin synthetic material that looks like interfacing called Trace-a-Pattern over the drawing and tracing the design with a felt-tip pen. The ink will transfer through the net onto the backing. Transfer pencils can be purchased from the suppliers listed on page 30. Trace-a-Pattern can be purchased in a fabric store.

Applying Binding

Sew two rows of machine stitching ¾ inch from the pattern edge. *Do not* cut off the excess burlap now. Sew nonadhesive twill binding to the line of the pattern edge. The free edge of the tape should face in toward the pattern. Ease the tape around the corners. The tape will be turned to the back later. When applying tape to a round rug, stretch the binding slightly to avoid excessive pleating when the tape is turned to the back. Tape color should match or harmonize with the background color of the rug. Pin binding tape to the excess burlap around the pattern as you work.

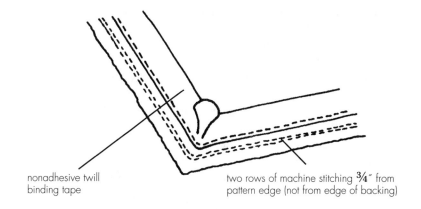

nonadhesive twill
binding tape

two rows of machine stitching ¾" from
pattern edge (not from edge of backing)

Color

With an adequate selection of colored wools you can hook your design in colors as they come directly from coats, skirts, or pants. Using tweeds, checks, and plaids along with solid colors will give texture and variety. Design motifs can be outlined in one color and filled with another color, or you may prefer to hook with all solid colors.

The general rules of color formation and combination are the same for artists and rug hookers. First, there are some terms you should be familiar with:

hue: the name of a color. To blend the hues red and blue will give another hue, violet.

value: the degree of light or darkness in a hue. Pink is a light value of red, and maroon is a dark value of red. A light value is also called a *tint,* and a dark value a *shade.* Pink and maroon are both values of the hue red.

intensity: the brightness or dullness of a hue. Value does not indicate intensity (brightness). While fire engine red has a higher intensity than maroon, and canary yellow is brighter than gold, violet in its dark value has a higher intensity than in lighter values.

primary colors: All colors are made from three colors called primaries: blue, yellow, and red. Other colors are combinations of these three hues.

secondary colors: Secondary colors are made by combining two primary colors. Red and yellow will produce orange; yellow and blue will yield green; and red and blue will give you purple. These combinations are secondary colors.

analogous colors: Colors that lie side by side on a color wheel. A group of analogous colors will contain one primary color and colors close to it. A warm analogous combination might be yellow (primary), yellow-orange, orange, yellow-green and green. A "cool" color combination might include green, blue (primary), blue violet, and violet.

complementary colors: Complementary colors lie opposite each other on a color wheel. When used side by side, complementary colors intensify each other. Red and green, blue and orange, yellow and violet—all are examples of complementary colors. Most high school and college colors are complementary combinations. It is not necessary to use the exact color opposite; analogous colors within a close range will achieve the same effect.

The Color Wheel

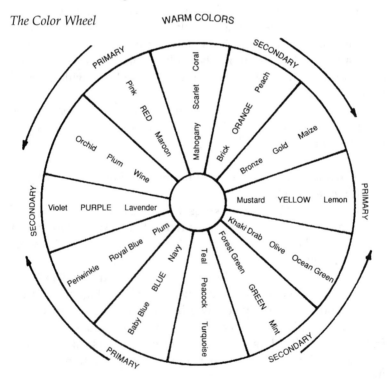

- 14 -

To add to this diversity (and confusion!) each color of your analogous color harmony and its complement can be used in its various values (shades and tints) and in varying intensities. All values and intensities of a color stand in the same relationship to other colors as their parent colors do.

In addition to your color choices, black, gray, light beiges, and off-whites are considered neutral and can be used in all color harmonies.

To keep a cool color scheme (greens, blues, violets) the cool colors must dominate. And within the cool colors themselves, one color must dominate. Pure blue may be too intense for large areas, so use it in small accents, dull it down, or use it as part of a tweed composed of blue and a neutral gray or beige. Green or blue-green could be the dominant color. Blue-violet is a little warmer due to the red in its makeup. Violet is warmer still and should be used carefully. Also violet, in its darker shades, is very intense.

Next choose a complement. All colors with red or yellow as part of their makeup are warm colors. Orange, the complement of blue, is a warm color. Since your main color decides the effect of your rug, and you want an overall effect of a cool rug, use the complement carefully and in much less quantity.

A good idea is to lay out your materials on the floor in the combinations they will occur in your rug—a lot of the background color and colors for large areas, with smaller amounts of the accent colors. See how you like the combinations.

A common mistake of beginners is to drift into the use of all medium values of colors. Many current home decorating ideas are attempts to duplicate the dull warm colors in heirloom quilts, hooked rugs, and embroideries that are found in folk art collections and museums. When these antiques were made, they were probably worked in bright colors. If you hook a rug today in all medium values, without any light, bright, or dark, in twenty-five years you will have trouble finding the design. Remember you are making your own heirloom. As a hooking teacher once said to me, "Time and grime will do the mellowing."

Along with color and design *texture* is also important. A rug hooked with materials of all the same weave and weight, such as wool flannel, lack the quality of texture and may be boring. Texture in a rug can be accomplished by using plaids, tweeds, checks, fuzzy or hard-surfaced materials, and closely woven or loosely woven materials. When wools are of different weights and weaves, the width of the strip used in hooking will have to be varied to be hooked evenly. A coat-weight material must be cut narrower than ¼-inch. A loose weave needs to be cut wider. This variation gives texture. Texture brings interest and diversity to your rug. It is more difficult to hook textured wools, but well worth the results.

Thoughts on Color Planning

- If a color combination looks great on paper but just doesn't look right on the rug, let it sit for awhile. Hook another part of the design. Come back to it later and if it still doesn't work, rip it out. Try another color combination.
- Keep it simple! You cannot use every color you like. Select two or three hues (colors) and various values and intensities of each.
- When you plan your design, plan to repeat colors over the surface of your rug to make your eye move and to hold the design together.
- Be creative with your colors. All leaves do not have to be green; all veins in leaves do not have to be gold or of a contrasting color of green. Take the red from a rose and use it for the vein in the rose leaf. All flowers do not have to be exactly their true colors. Train your eye to look for color combinations in magazines, paintings, and nature.
- Do not use bright whites.
- Use neutral colors to tone down and relate colors.
- For texture, use tweeds and loose weaves, etc., containing your chosen colors.
- For assistance in color planning: Grumbacher's Color Computer Wheel is available at artist supply or paint stores.

Hooking Technique

Insert the backing into an embroidery hoop or fasten with long tacks to a wooden frame. Try to keep the backing taut while keeping the grain of the backing straight. If using thumb tacks, make a tuck in the backing to prevent tearing or making a large hole in the backing.

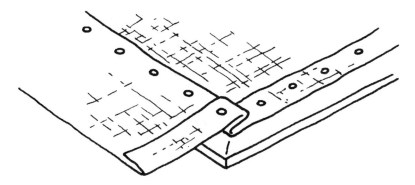

Begin to hook in the center of the pattern. Grasp the hook firmly in the right hand as shown in the illustration. Reverse the procedure if you are lefthanded. The hook should always be turned up to enter the backing to scoop up a wool strip. To begin to hook, hold a strip of wool in the left hand underneath the backing.

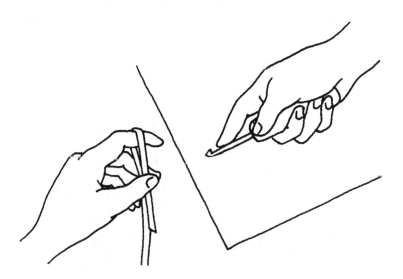

From the upper side of the backing push the hook through an opening between the threads of the backing.

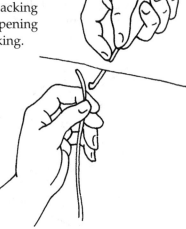

Pick up the end of the strip and pull one inch of the strip to the top side.

Skip two threads and make a second stitch, bringing up a loop instead of an end. A good loop height is ¼ inch to ⅜ inch. Continue making loops until the strip is finished.

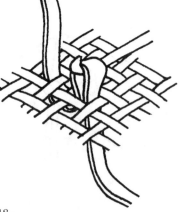

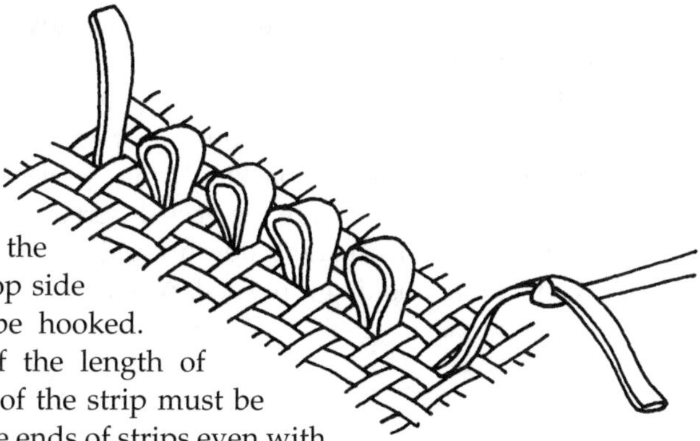

Bring the end of the
strip through to the top side
in the next hole to be hooked.
Always, regardless of the length of
strip used, both ends of the strip must be
on the top side. Cut the ends of strips even with
the loops.

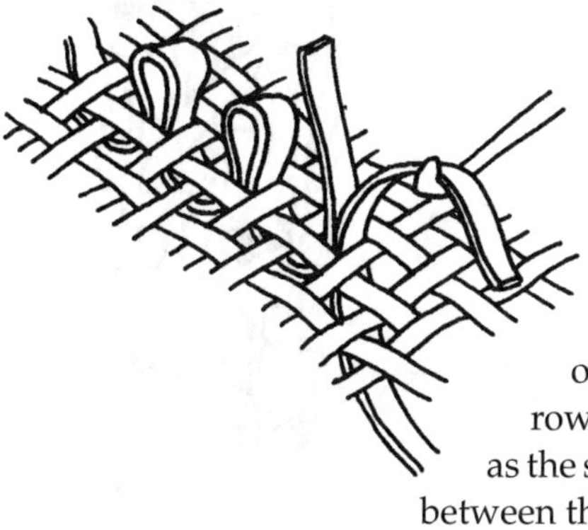

Begin the second strip by
pulling the beginning end up
in the same hole with the end
of the first strip. If possible, keep
rows two threads apart the same
as the stitches, and stagger the stitches
between the stitches of the previous row.

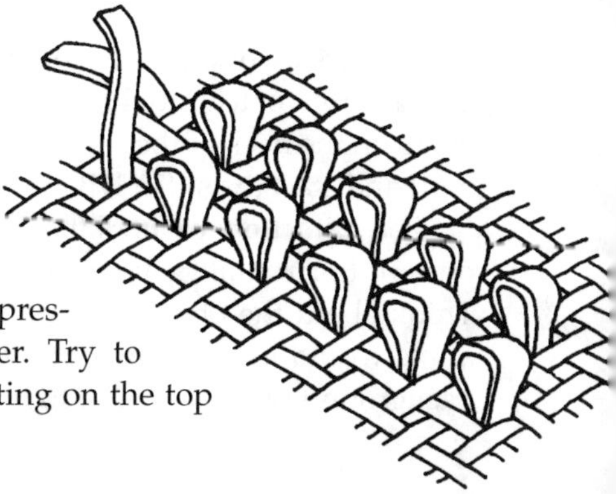

Continue to hook one row
against the other following the
contour of the previous row. The
loops stay in place because of the pres-
sure of one loop against the other. Try to
make the loops even, with no twisting on the top
of your rug.

Avoid packing the foundation too tightly. Crowding is a common problem for beginners. On the face of the rug the loops should touch at the top with no backing showing. On the underside some backing should show. Turn over your rug periodically to check for large patches of unhooked backing (impossible to see from the front) called "windows." From the back, insert a toothpick through the unhooked area. Turn right side up and the toothpick will point out where more hooking is needed. Also check your rug periodically for suppleness.

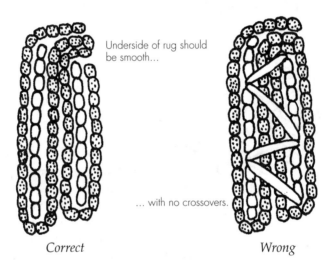

Underside of rug should be smooth...

... with no crossovers.

Correct   *Wrong*

The underside of the rug should be smooth, with no ends or lumps and no large patches of backing showing. There should be no crossovers on the back of the rug. Bring the end of the strip to the top, cut it off and start the stitch with a new strip.

The direction of hooking should follow the contours of the design: horizontal or vertical for a house, or curved for an apple. Think about the object you are hooking. Horizontal hooking in an apple would look funny. After your motif is hooked, hook a line of background wool around it to firm up its lines.

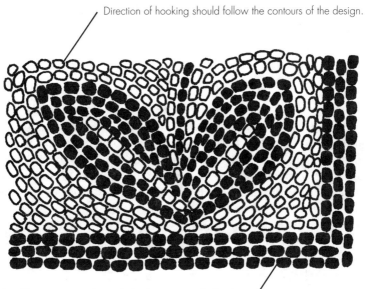

Direction of hooking should follow the contours of the design.

Work at least two rows of straight hooking next to the binding.

Large areas of background hooking can be done in several ways: with horizontal or vertical lines, or with random filling-in by marking a few wavy lines or large S's with a felt-tip pen on the backing, hooking these lines, and then filling in between them. However, at least two rows of straight hooking should be done next to the binding.

Thoughts on Hooking Technique

- Do not hook on the lines of the pattern. Stay within. If hooked on the line, your motif will be one row larger all around.
- When you have all the wool together for hooking your rug, including background and design, divide it into four groups. Now mentally divide your rug into four sections. While hooking, if you run out of wool for one section, it will mean you do not have enough for the other three sections either. Do not borrow from the other piles. You will have to get more wool of the same color or dye more wool.

Finishing and Care

Finishing

After you have completed your hooked article, cut off the excess backing at the row of stitching ¾ inch from the pattern edge. Turn binding and burlap to the back. The tape should cover the raw edge of the burlap. Press with a steam iron as you turn the edge back. Miter the corners and pin. Use carpet/button thread and a strong needle to hand stitch the binding to the backing. The stitches should attach to the backing and the wool strips in the backing. Do not sew through to the front. The binding can be pulled back all the way or a ¼ inch edge of binding with burlap underneath can be allowed to show on the outer edge. This helps the edge to wear better. Never apply any latex coating to the back of the rug.

Lay the rug face down on a padded floor and thoroughly steam press with a damp towel. The rug will feel damp. Press again lightly, with a towel, the top surface. Let it lie overnight or until the rug is dry.

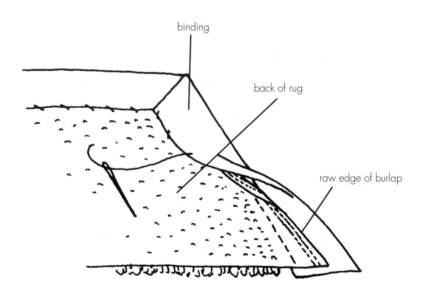

binding

back of rug

raw edge of burlap

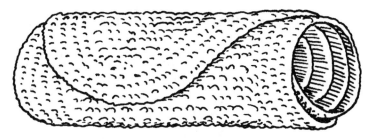

For storage, always roll your rug with the pattern facing out.

Care of the Hooked Article

On the floor, a pad underneath the rug will improve wearability and looks. It will also help to keep the rug from slipping. To clean a hooked rug, vacuum with low suction or sweep carefully with a broom. Do not shake. For more serious soil, clean as any other good-quality rug by using a rug shampoo after first testing the colorfastness. *Do not wash in an automatic washing machine.*

In times past, before commercial rug cleaners, women took their rugs outside after a snowfall and swept snow over the surface to freshen and clean the rug. During routine daily use, the woman of the house might turn the rug over and have the underside on view. This saved the top. It also encouraged the dirt and grit near the backing to loosen and fall out. Besides, the underside is attractive, too.

For storing, always roll the rug with the pattern facing out. It puts much less strain on the backing. For long storage, sprinkle moth crystals or moth-repellent herbs in the rolled rug. Wrap a cloth such as a sheet around the rolled rug. Do not use plastic: the rug is all-natural fibers and needs to breathe. Store away from extreme dry heat and excessive moisture.

Dyeing Woolens

Perhaps in the future when you are planning a rug, you will not have just the right color to do a particular section. The only way to get it is to dye your wool. Dyeing has a reputation for being messy and time-consuming. It is a little of both! But it can be satisfying and fun too.

Natural Dyeing

Natural dyeing is done with weeds, berries, barks, etc. Naturally dyed colors are beautiful, and almost without exception compatible. The process is very time-consuming and must be done at specific times of the year as plants yield their best dyes at different times on their growing cycle. All natural dyestuffs have their own personalities and require an individualized approach. (See the reading list on page 30.)

Commercial Dyes and Dyeing Equipment

Dyeing with commercial dyes can be done with equipment found in your kitchen, a hardware store, or at a flea market. You will need a 10-quart or 12-quart stainless steel or enamel pot (white is best), a flat pan 3 to 4 inches high and approximately 12 by 15 inches wide, gloves, tongs, aluminum foil, measuring cup, measuring spoons, pint jars, detergent, uniodized salt, and white vinegar. Cushing's Perfection Dyes are generally used by rug hookers. The selection is large and the quality is excellent. They are available from the suppliers listed on page 30.

Do not use copper, aluminum, or tin pots: the dyes will react with the metals and affect the colors. My favorite pots are porcelain enamel refrigerator crispers from old discarded refrigerators. Because they are white, you can see how the dye is being absorbed, and they are easily cleaned. White enamel buckets are very good also.

WARNING: *Keep your dyeing utensils separate from personal cooking pots. Keep all dry dyes and dye solutions out of the reach of children. Dyeing should be done in a well-ventilated place, wearing a disposable face mask and rubber gloves. Clean up spills carefully, especially if you must dye in a food preparation area. (Spread newspapers over exposed surfaces.)*

Each dye package contains two teaspoons of dry dye and instructions for use. Ignore these instructions. They are for dyeing large pieces of wool up to one pound in weight. You will be dyeing small pieces of wool and using amounts of dry dye measuring from a few grains to ¼ teaspoon. Once opened, dry dye will absorb moisture from the atmosphere. Therefore it is a good idea to keep your dry dye packages in a plastic container.

When making dye solutions, use boiling water and a measuring cup. Put the designated amount of dry dye in the measuring cup. Add the proper amount of boiling water (usually one cup). Stir until all dye is dissolved. If you are not going to use all this solution in one session, pour it into pint jars with screw tops. These can be kept in a cool place (out of the reach of children) for years. Mayonnaise jars are excellent. Label the jars with the name of the dye, amount of dry dye used, amount of water, and the date. You think you will remember the dye used and the date, but a month from now you will not. And dyes in solution tend to look alike; it is hard to tell a bronze-green from an olive green. If a solution becomes thickened while in storage, it can be restored by bringing it to a boil.

Record Keeping

Keeping a record of your dyeing results is important as well as interesting. Before dyeing your wools, cut off a ½" x 2" piece of each wool to be dyed. Along with this snippet of wool write down the exact amount of dye solution used. On the jar label it will say how much dry dye is in the dye solution. This information is necessary to duplicate the dye solution in case that too needs to be replenished. The original wool snippet is also useful for comparison in whatever dye process you do. Is the new color dark enough? Has enough color been removed? Is it dull enough? The most important reason for record keeping is to duplicate colors if you run out of a color before the rug is finished. With that snippet of original wool and the name and amount of the dye or dyes used to get the color, you will be able to make more of the color you need. It may not be exactly the same, but when intermingled with the previously dyed wool, the difference will not be noticeable. When the wool is dyed and dried, cut off another ½" x 2" piece of wool. Staple these two small snippets of wool, one the original and the other the dyed one, side by side on an index card or in a notebook with an explanation of the dyes used.

Marrying or Blending Colors

In your collection of used wools, you may have a group of materials, including solids, textures, and plaids, that are mostly green but too different to be used together for a green background. The colors of these wools can be blended. Immerse your assorted wools including some beiges and neutral grays in a pot of water to which 2 tablespoons of detergent have been added. One-half pound or less is the best amount to work with. Do not cram. Bring to a boil. Turn down to simmer.

As the wools simmer, you will see color bleeding out of them. Allow to "stew" for 15 minutes. Add ⅓ cup of white vinegar to the water. Continue to simmer for 30 minutes. The color will be taken up evenly by all the wools, and the water will be clear or nearly clear. After 30 minutes, remove the wools from the water and rinse several times in clear water to remove all excess color and vinegar. Dry the wool in a dryer or on a line. Intermingling this assortment while hooking will result in an attractive marbleized background.

White vinegar and uniodized salt are mordants, which set the dyes in the wools and help the wools to take up the colors. Salt generally dulls the colors while vinegar brightens them.

Pots must be scoured carefully after each dyeing session. If any color remains in the pot, it will affect the results the next time you dye, particularly if you are dyeing a light color.

Removing Color

If you want to lighten or decrease the intensity (brightness) of a color, some dye must be removed. Simmer the wool in water and two tablespoons of detergent until sufficient color has been bled out. Compare to the snippet of original wool. If it is still not light enough, discard the water, put the wools into fresh water and detergent, and simmer again. It may be necessary to repeat this process several times to get the desired value. When you are satisfied with the color, put the wool into fresh warm water, add ⅓ cup vinegar, and simmer 30 minutes. Rinse thoroughly and dry. The color will now be set.

Dulling Colors

If you have too bright a color, removing some color by simmering in water and detergent can help. But many times it will change the value of the color when all you wanted to do was to take away some of the intensity (brightness). Adding black dye, or the complement of the color you are working with, is another way to dull the color. Kelly green is a beautiful color, but in a rug it jumps right out at you. By adding a little red dye (the complement of green), the color will be dulled or grayed.

To add a "little bit of dry dye" to a dye bath, moisten the end of a toothpick in a pot of hot water. Add the presoaked wool. These few grains of dye may be enough to dull the wool to the intensity you want. Be careful with the amount used, as too much red will dull the green more than you want and ultimately turn it gray. Since you wish to dull a color, use ⅓ cup of salt as a mordant. The color of the wool will be darker when wet. With a gloved hand, squeeze the water out of a small portion of the wool to better see what it will look like dry. If the wool is not sufficiently dulled and the dye pot is clear of dye, add a few more grains. When you are satisfied with the color, simmer for 30 minutes to set. Rinse thoroughly and dry. The same procedure can be followed using black dye.

Overdyeing

Material can be overdyed without removing the original color. By overdyeing yellow wool with blue dye solution, the wool will be colored green. A great variety of colors can be produced, always keeping in mind how the original color will affect the resulting color. To overdye your chosen wools, a dye solution is needed. A good proportion is ¼ teaspoon dry dye to 1 cup of boiling water. If the dye is for a light color such as peach, more dry dye could be used. Remember, however, you cannot overdye a dark color with a light dye to achieve a lighter color. The dyed color will be no lighter than the original wool.

Use ½ pound or less of wool at one time. Presoak in warm water with a tablespoon of dishwashing liquid. This enables the dye to be better and more evenly absorbed. Put the drained, but not rinsed, wool into a pot of warm water. Holding the wool to the side with tongs, add one or two teaspoons of dye solution to the pot and bring to a boil. Add a mordant of either ⅓ cup of vinegar or ⅓ cup of salt and simmer. The dye color will be taken up into the wool. Add more dye solution in small amounts; it is easier to add color than it is to remove it. When judging depth of color, be aware that wool always appears darker when wet. With tongs, lift a piece of wool out of the dye pot. With a gloved hand squeeze out the excess water. Examine in good light. If you are satisfied with the color, simmer 30 minutes, rinse thoroughly, and dry.

Antique Black

To achieve an antique black, which is great for backgrounds, especially for a Victorian feel, simmer together a group of dark-colored wools. Include all types — plaids, textures, greens, browns, reds, dark grays, and a small piece of black. For antique black with a greenish tinge, add some bronze-green dye. Proceed as you did in the section on blending. The results will give you a mottled background.

Dyeing Tips

- Dye is what is in the dye package; dye solution is water with dye dissolved in it.
- The amount of water in the dye pot has no affect on dye results. The only thing that matters is the amount of dye in the dye pot. The water is merely a vehicle to get the dye into the fabric.
- Black wool almost always appears too dark and too flat unless some color is removed.
- Take the time to keep a dyeing record.
- Always wash your wool before using even if it is not to be dyed.
- To lightly dull a too-bright white wool, use a very small amount of taupe, ecru, or khaki drab dye.
- Keep the wools from each dyeing session together with large pin, a metal shower curtain ring, or next best, a clear plastic bag, while working on your project. If not all used, keep together for storage. That way you will have related colors together.
- Store your wools separately by color. For visibility, clear biodegradable trash bags are great. Do not seal the tops: wool needs to breathe.
- If you have a craft/work room, put your dyed wool pieces in their related colors on large pins. Attach these pins to metal shower curtain rings on a rod across an end of your room. Instant decorating and instant visibility when you are looking for that special color!
- Relax and enjoy dyeing. There are no mistakes; only surprises!

Appendices

I. Additional Reading

Adrosko, Rita. *Natural Dyes and Home Dyeing*
    (Dover Publications, 1971)
Batchelder, Martha. *The Art of Hooked-Rug Making*
    (Down East Books, 1983)
Beatty, Alice, and Mary Sargent. *Basic Rug Hooking*
    (Stackpole Books, 1990)
Ebi, Dotti. *Scraps or Spots—Dyeing to reuse old wools*
    (Dotti Ebi, 1979) Available through suppliers.
Kopp, Joel and Kate. *American Hooked and Sewn Rugs*
    (E.P. Dutton Inc., 1985)
Moshimer, Joan. *Complete Book of Rug Hooking*
    (Dover Publications, 1989)
Rex, Stella Hay. *Choice Hooked Rugs and Practical Hooked
    Rugs* (Prentice Hall, 1953; Persea Books, 1975)
Tynan, Jean. *Dyeing for Primitive Rug Hooking*
    (Jean Tynan, 1984)

Rug Hooking (print and online magazine)
    877-462-2604; *www.rughookingonline.com*

II. Suppliers

DiFranza Designs
    978-664-2034; *www.difranzadesigns.com*
    Hooking supplies, patterns, kits
Fredericksburg Rugs
    866-934-6273; *www.fredericksburgrugs.com*
    Hooking supplies, patterns, kits, dyes, books
Harry M. Fraser Co.
    336-573-9830; *www.fraserrugs.com*
    Hooking supplies, cloth backs, books and videos
Past & Present Rug Shop
    902-963-2453; *www.hookamat.com*
    Hooking supplies, patterns, kits
W. Cushing & Company
    800-626-7847; *www.wcushing.com*
    Hooking supplies, books, kits, Perfection dyes

III. Rug Hooking Camps

Rug-hooking camps are gatherings of beginning and advanced rug hookers to enjoy hooking and fellowship under the guidance of experienced teachers in all types and phases of hooking. The camps run for a few days to a week. The location of the camp could be a college, a school, a nature center with dormitories, a private home, or a hotel by the sea. Room and board and tuition are usually included in one fee.

If you are lucky enough to live near a rug-hooking supplier, ask them for recommendations. Otherwise, start your search at Rug Hooking Online, Rug Hooking magazine's Web site. Read through the Links page to find rug-hooking business that offer camps and retreats.

IV. Hooking Organizations

There are many rug-hooking guilds, with chapter and members worldwide. Two active groups are

The Association of Traditional Hooking Artists
www.atharugs.com

The Green Mountain Rug Hooking Guild
617-945-2318; *www.gmrhg.org*

V. Rug Exhibits

Throughout the country, small hooking groups have shows exhibiting their recently hooked rugs. Sometimes their hooking teachers will have an exhibition of students' work. Usually these are held in a local meeting hall or church and will last only a few days. These shows will sometimes be combined with hooking workshops. Look for announcements in your local newspaper or *Rug Hooking* magazine.

Many city and town museums have hooked rugs in their collections. A few may be on permanent display. Others may be shown as part of another presentation. In 1974, the Museum of American Folk Art in New York City had a landmark exhibition devoted exclusively to hooked rugs. The book *American Hooked and Sewn Rugs* by the curators, Joel and Kate Kopp, is a result of that show. The Bybee Collection at the Dallas Art Museum, Texas, has a good collection of hooked rugs. Hopefully, as hooked rugs gain in popularity, more museums will include them in their textile collections and exhibitions.

Hooked rugs have been seen on the floors in period rooms of living history museums. The Henry Ford Museum in Dearborn, Michigan; Winterthur in Wilmington, Delaware; and Old Sturbridge Village in Sturbridge, Massachusetts, have good collections. Smaller living history museums, such as Landis Valley Museum in Lancaster, Pennsylvania have hooked rugs, too. Since exhibits rotate, contact the museum before you go to find out what is on display.

One outstanding permanent collection can be seen at the Shelburne Museum in Shelburne, Vermont; additionally, many properties in the Society for the Preservation of New England Antiquities (SPNEA) have hooked rugs in their collections.

Shelburne Museum
    802-985-3346; *www.shelburnemuseum.org*

Historic New England
    www.historicnewengland.org